C000180102

POPULAR
PRAYERS

Cover picture:
From a Wood Carving by Philip Lindsey Clark at Aylesford
Illustration by Alex Jardine

Printed by A.G.A. Printers & Sons
Unit H4, Shipyard Industrial Estate,
Upper Brents, Faversham, Kent ME13 7DZ
Telephone: 01795 533295

First Published 2003
Saint Albert's Press
Whitefriars, 34 Tanners Street
Faversham, Kent, ME13 7JN, U.K

© British Province of Carmelites
ISBN: 0-904849-24-4

BRITISH PROVINCE OF CARMELITES

The Order of Carmelites, or Brethren of the Blessed Virgin of Mount Carmel developed from a group of lay hermits living a contemplative life modelled on Elijah and Our Lady, in 12th century Palestine. We first came to Britain in 1242. As the hermits became friars following the 1247 General Chapter in Aylesford, and later in 1452 when nuns and lay people were formally admitted to the Order, the Carmelites developed their distinctive mission of following in the footsteps of Jesus through prayer, ministry and service.

Britain was the largest Carmelite Province in the Order until its suppression at the Reformation. It was re-established under the patronage of Our Lady of the Assumption in the twentieth century. There are currently seven communities of friars, three of sisters and many local groups of Lay Carmelites in Britain. Members of the Carmelite Family seek the face of the Living God in parishes, prisons, university chaplaincies, retreat centres and through many other forms of ministry.

To find out more about the Carmelites, why not visit one of our websites:

British Carmelite Websites

Province website
www.carmelite.org

Aylesford website
www.thefriars.org.uk

Faversham website
www.stjudeshrine.org.uk

PRAYER

Prayer is religion in action. The Christian, who tries to be a real Christian, learns to live his prayer and to pray his life. In the words of the fourth eucharistic prayer, his life becomes a 'living sacrifice of praise'. This 'living sacrifice of praise' means quite simply saying 'Yes' to God day after day in the events of life. Saying 'Yes' to life, to the people among whom we live and work, to the society of which we are a part. But that 'Yes' will scarcely ring true unless we have already said it in the depths of our hearts in personal prayer. We cannot pray all of the time, everywhere, unless we bother to pray some of the time, somewhere.

Praying to God some of the time, somewhere, demands a time and a place. It may be a very short period of time, a few minutes at the end of a very demanding day. The place itself may not always be conducive to prayer. If we have little privacy in our lives, the place may well be in our own hearts amid the noise and bustle of the city. Perhaps, as St Teresa of Avila suggested, we may have to find God among the pots and pans in the kitchen.

The prayers you will find in this prayer book are prayers for all occasions, prayers for the ups and downs of life. Or, as St Thérèse of Lisieux puts it, they are 'a cry of grateful love from the crest of joy or the trough of despair.'

Some occasions, more than others, move us to deep personal prayer. The death of someone we love, a country devastated by war or famine, the suffering of the innocent, can force us, like Job, to ask the most fundamental questions about life and its purpose. Such events confront us with mystery. We have no answer. We can only say to God that his ways are not our ways. We can only ask him to give us patience with his ways.

But the birth of a baby leads us to prayer of another kind. So does the sight of a young couple at the altar making their marriage promises to each other with evident sincerity and wholeheartedness. We come before the wonder of new life, of new love.

Comings and goings, separations and engagements, the reunion of friends, setting out on a journey, all give us food for thought and prayer. We read the book of life, the book of nature, of events and of persons. We reflect and we pray. Reading, thinking, praying, are the three steps in our education in prayer. When we read the book of life in what happens and in what people say and do in the everyday world, we never have all the answers. But we do have a vision of God and of life. In prayer, all that we experience can be illuminated by that vision and lead us deeper into its mystery. Hence, in prayer we work with God who ever seeks to transform us by the power of his Spirit into the likeness of his Son.

The Christian vision and experience of God is written large for us in the pages of the bible, that story of God's dealings with his people, which is our story too. The God of Abraham, 'our father in faith', is the God of Jesus whom we call 'Father'. As he taught his people of old he still teaches us today. For the Christian, the Bible is a treasure house of prayer. The utterances of men and women of old, the spontaneous prayers from the heart, the accumulated wisdom of a people living in close intimacy with the saving God, the prayer of Christ himself and his teaching on prayer, and the beautiful outpourings from the heart of St Paul, all these should teach us to pray, simply and from the heart.

The Bible and the liturgical ritual serve to remind us of the moods of prayer which we can so often ignore or express in the wrong way. The mood of petition is the kind of prayer that helps us to get it all together. Petition is accepting: accepting ourselves, our world and its people. Intercession is being concerned about others, a release from preoccupation with ourselves. St Paul is forever telling the early Christians to praise and to give thanks constantly. He is telling them to make their lives a continuous eucharist.

The high point of the Christian's daily eucharist effort is the Sunday eucharist. Here, the weekly coming together of the Christian family gives us added inspiration for praise and thanksgiving. The liturgy of the word gives us fresh motivation, Sunday after Sunday; for joyful thanksgiving. This weekly gathering also sends us back to our daily surroundings. Our Sunday Eucharist feeds our daily prayer and inspires our saying 'Yes' to God in the events of life. There is no conflict then between daily living, personal prayer and the liturgy. The word of Christ to which we listen at Sunday Mass dwells in us richly for the rest of the week and strengthens us to 'do everything in the name of the Lord Jesus giving thanks to God the Father through him' (Col 3: 17)

Eltin Griffin, O.Carm.

PRAYERS IN COMMON USE

Our Father (The Lord's Prayer)

OUR Father, who art in heaven, hallowed be thy name. Thy kingdom come. Thy will be done on earth, as it is in heaven. Give us this day our daily bread, and forgive us our trespasses, as we forgive those who trespass against us, and lead us not into temptation, but deliver us from evil.   Amen.

A Modern Lord's Prayer

OUR Father in Heaven, let your holy name be known, let your kingdom come, and your will be done, on earth as in heaven. Give us today the bread that we need, and forgive us our wrongs, as we forgive those who have done wrong to us. Do not lead us into trial, but save us from evil.   Amen

Hail Mary

HAIL, Mary, full of grace, the Lord is with thee: blessed art thou among women, and blessed is the fruit of thy womb, Jesus. Holy Mary, Mother of God, pray for us sinners, now, and at the hour of our death.   Amen

G LORY be to the Father, and to the Son, and to the Holy Spirit.
As it was in the beginning, is now, and ever shall be, world without end.   Amen

MORNING PRAYER

Each day can be a new beginning. Yesterday is past, tomorrow has not happened, today is the here and now in which we live. Morning is the time to open our eyes anew to God's world and to become aware once again of our Father who is continually at work within us through his Spirit forming us in the likeness of his Son.

There may be little time for morning prayer, but the essential thing is that we turn to God, however briefly, with all our heart and awake to his loving and strengthening presence. The following prayers suggest some thoughts for morning prayer. It is for each of us to choose what suits best, remembering that the words of prayer have meaning only when they come from the heart.

O my God, you love me,
    You are with me night and day.
I want to love you always
In all I do and say.
I'll try to please you, Father,
Bless me throughout the day.   Amen

O JESUS,
    through the most pure heart of Mary,
I offer you all my thoughts,
words and actions,
joys and sufferings,
of this day
for all the intentions
of your most divine heart.

I expect to pass through this world
but once; any good, therefore,
that I can do, or kindness that I
can show to any fellow-creature,
let me do it now; let me
not defer or neglect it, for I shall not
pass this way again.

Tobit 3:11; Ps 5:3

You are blessed, O God of mercy!
May your name be blessed for ever,
and may all things you have made
bless you everlastingly.
It is you whom I invoke, O Lord.
In the morning you hear me;
in the morning I offer you my prayer,
watching and waiting.

The Benedictus
The Canticle of Zechariah Lk1:68-79

BLESSED be the Lord, the God of Israel!
He has visited his people and redeemed them.

He has raised up for us a mighty saviour
in the house of David his servant,
as he promised by the lips of holy men,
those who were his prophets from of old.

A saviour who would free us from our foes,
from the hands of all who hate us.
So his love for our fathers is fulfilled
and his holy covenant remembered.

He swore to Abraham our father to grant us,
that free from fear, and saved from the hands of our foes,
we might serve him in holiness and justice
all the days of our life in his presence.

As for you, little child,
you shall be called a prophet of God, the Most High.
You shall go ahead of the Lord
to prepare his ways before him,

To make known to his people their salvation
through forgiveness of all their sins,
the loving-kindness of the heart of our God
who visits us like the dawn from on high.

He will give light to those in darkness,
those who dwell in the shadow of death,
and guide us into the way of peace.

Divine Office

VISIT, we beseech thee, O Lord,
our homes and families,
and drive far from them all the snares
of the enemy; let your holy angels
dwell herein to keep us in peace,
and may your blessing be
always upon us.
Through Christ Our Lord.   Amen.
Prayer from Compline

NOW as we retire to rest,
guard us by your grace and let
our sleep renew in us the strength
and courage to serve you
faithfully tomorrow and
the rest of our lives.   Amen.

The Magnificat
The Canticle of Mary Lk1:46-55

MY soul glorifies the Lord,
   my spirit rejoices in God, my Saviour.
He looks on his servant in her lowliness;
henceforth all ages will call me blessed.

The Almighty works marvels for me.
Holy his name!
His mercy is from age to age,
on those who fear him.

He puts forth his arm in strength
and scatters the proud-hearted.
He casts the mighty from their thrones
and raises the lowly.

He fills the starving with good things,
sends the rich away empty.

He protects Israel, his servant,
remembering his mercy,
the mercy promised to our fathers,
to Abraham and his sons for ever.

Divine Office

NIGHT PRAYER

Night prayer gathers together the day with all that it has brought of joy and of sorrow, of interest and of boredom, of good and of evil. All this we offer to God, confident that we can place ourselves with entire trust in the hands of his loving mercy. As we enter the little death of sleep we can make the great prayer of the dying Jesus, 'Father, into your hands I commend my spirit.' In this way our night prayer turns us towards a new day, a new beginning and a new resurrection.

The Nunc Dimittis
The Canticle of Simeon Lk 2:29-32

AT last, all-powerful Master,
    you give leave to your servant
to go in peace, according to your promise.

For my eyes have seen your salvation
which you have prepared for all nations,
the light to enlighten the gentiles
and give glory to Israel, your people.

Divine Office

A Child's Night Prayer

GOD, I have spent a happy day.
I worked happily.
I played happily, thanks to you.
Now I am going to sleep.
Guard me and all the children of the world.
We are in your care.
You hear us when we call, so I shall sleep well.
Thank you, God.   Amen.

Night Prayer

GOD, our Father, I come to say
thank you for your love today.
Thank you for my family
and all the friends you give to me.
Guard me in the dark of night
and in the morning send your light.   Amen

Night Prayer of Carmel

DEAR Mother of Carmel, we ask you to commend to your divine Son all the cares and anxieties of those who have asked our prayers. Succour and restore the suffering in body and mind, pity those who are tried by ill health and disease, give them light in darkness and, in your great compassion for the afflicted and unhappy, lead them close to the strength of Jesus Christ, your Son, our Lord.

We commend to your safe keeping our parents, relatives, and friends and all who have done good to us for the sake of your holy name. Guard them from temptation and surprise and keep them from evil and misfortune.

At your feet may we learn the true spirit of Carmel. May our hearts burn with the zeal of St. Elias; we implore the childlike trust in you of St. Simon Stock; we would crave the undaunted desires of St. Teresa, the mystic love born of suffering of St. John of the Cross and St. Mary Magdalen de Pazzi, the courage and shining purity of St. Albert and St. Andrew. In simplicity with St. Thérèse may our souls grow in trust and deepen in love.

We ask you for vocations: lead other sons and daughters into your land of Carmel. Be our right hand in our weakness: give us greater trust in your promise of blessing and protection: ever renew in us the true spirit of our vocation: desert not your own; give us courage to build anew; quicken our desire to grow and increase and grant us good success.

Let us give God thanks for all his gracious gifts. Blessed be the Most Holy Trinity. May holy Mary and all the angels and saints of God be praised now and for evermore.   Amen.

Prayer of St. Francis

LORD make me an instrument of your peace,
     Where there is hatred,
     let me sow love,
     Where there is injury, pardon,
     Where there is darkness, light,
     Where there is sadness, joy,
     Where there is doubt, faith,
     And where there is despair, hope.

     O divine master,
     grant that I may not so much seek
     To be consoled, as to console,
     To be understood, as to understand,
     To be loved, as to love

               For,
It is in giving that we receive,
It is in forgiving that we are pardoned,
And it is in dying that we are born
to eternal life.

Dedication of Service

T EACH us, good Lord,
   to serve you as you deserve;
To give and not to count the cost;
To fight and not to heed the wounds;
To toil and not to seek for rest;
To labour and not to seek reward,
Save that of knowing we do your will.
Through Jesus Christ Our Lord.   Amen.

St. Ignatius

L ORD. Thou knowest
   I shall be verie busie this day.
I may forget thee.
Do not thou forget me.

Lord Astley before the battle of Edgehill.

ALMIGHTY GOD,
Your only-begotten Son, Jesus
went down to Nazareth and was subject
to Mary and Joseph.
Help me to follow his example
of obedience and service
in my own family.

MAY I be a source of comfort
to my parents.
May I honour them and appreciate
the sacrifices they make for me.
Reward them a hundredfold.
Guide and help them
at all times.
May my family live in happiness
and unity in this world
and be reunited in the
eternal happiness of heaven in the next.
Through Christ Our Lord.   Amen.

A prayer for our homes and for those whom we love

O GOD, our Father,
     by whose will we
live together in families,
let your blessing rest upon
our homes and those we love.
Bless our parents and
the members of our families.
Give them health and
strength of soul and body,
and unite us all in
love of you.
Through Christ our Lord.   Amen.

L ORD JESUS,
     perfect model of all that a
Christian should be like.
Be with me always,
at home, at school, at play.
Grant that I may be
prepared to do my duty and
to show loyalty to all people,
clean in thought word and
deed, and always willing
to serve you.   Amen.

RELATIONSHIPS are difficult,
    Lord, and sometimes I find it hard
to get on with *N*.
What he/she does and says
often angers me.
Help me to see his/her good points.
He/She is made by you,
dear to you, loved by you.
Give me the grace
to see him/her as a friend
and to be especially kind to him/her
next time we meet.   Amen.

Prayer for the Sick

LORD Jesus,
    who went about doing good and healing all,
we ask you to bless your friends who are sick.
Give them strength in body, courage in spirit,
and patience with pain.
Let them recover their health,
So that, restored to the Christian community,
they may joyfully praise your name.
For you live and reign for ever and ever.

                              Amen.

GUIDE and strengthen me, Holy Spirit,
      in trying to accomplish
the mission in life
you have assigned to me.
You haven't exactly made it easy,
but when I think
of the trials of your martyrs,
I stop complaining.
I want to honour you,
do some good for a lot of people,
and then rest with you for a long time.

                                        Amen.

WE pray Lord,
    that our actions
may be prompted by
your holy inspirations and
furthered by your
gracious assistance:
so that every prayer and
work of ours
may always begin
from you and
through you be happily ended.
Through Christ Our Lord.   Amen.

DIVINE OFFICE

I ask not to see . . .
    I ask not to know . . .
I ask simply to be used . . .
                    Cardinal Newman

SOUL of Christ, be my sanctification
Body of Christ, be my salvation
Blood of Christ, fill all my veins
Water from Christ's side, wash out my stains
Passion of Christ, my comfort be
O good Jesus, listen to me
In thy wounds I fain would hide
Ne'er to be parted from thy side
Guard me should the foe assail me
Call me when my life shall fail me
Bid me come to thee above
With thy saints to sing thy love
World without end.   Amen.

Poetic text by Cardinal Newman
Original sometimes attributed to St. Ignatius of Loyola

Prayer after Holy Communion

THANKS to you my Lord Jesus Christ . . .

for all the benefits which you have given me,
for all the pains and insults which you have borne
for me.

O most merciful redeemer, friend and brother,

May I know you more clearly,
Love you more dearly,
And follow you more nearly.

St. Richard of Chichester d. 1253

Meditation When Someone Has Died

WE seem to give them back to you, O God,
who gave them to us. Yet, as you did
not lose them in giving, so do we not
lose them by their return. Not as the world
gives, do you give, O lover of souls.
What you give, you do not take away, for
what is yours is ours also if we are
yours. And life is eternal and love is immortal,
and death is only an horizon, and an
horizon is nothing save the limit of our sight.
Lift us up, strong Son of God, that we
may see more clearly; draw us closer to yourself
that we may know ourselves to be nearer
to our loved ones who are with you. And while
you prepare a place for us, prepare
us also for that happy place, that where
you are, we may be also for evermore.   Amen.

William Penn

GOD give me the GRACE
    to accept the things I cannot change,
the COURAGE to change the things I can,
And
The WISDOM to know the difference.

LET nothing disturb thee
    Nothing affright thee
All things are passing
        Patience gains all.
Who serves God, wants for nothing
He alone is sufficient.

St. Teresa of Jesus

The Serenity Prayer

GOD, grant me the serenity
to accept the things
I cannot change,

Courage to change the
things I can, and the
wisdom to know the difference.

Living one day at a time;

Enjoying one moment at a time;
Accepting hardship as the
pathway to peace.

Taking, as he did, this
sinful world as it is,
not as I would have it.

Trusting that he will make
all things right if I
surrender to his will;

That I may be reasonably happy
in this life, and supremely
happy with him forever in
the next.   Amen

Reinhold Neibuhr - 1926

Footprints

ONE night I dreamed I was walking along the beach with the Lord.

Many scenes from my life flashed across the sky.

In each scene I noticed footprints in the sand.

Sometimes there were two sets of footprints.

Other times there were one set of footprints.

This bothered me because I noticed that during the low periods of my life

When I was suffering from anguish, sorrow, or defeat,

I could see only one set of footprints.

So I said to the Lord, "you promised me, Lord, that if I followed you,
    you would walk with me always.

But I noticed that during the most trying periods of my life

there have only been one set of prints in the sand.

Why, when I have needed you most, you have not been there for me?"

The Lord replied,

"The times when you have seen only one set of footprints

are when I carried you."

Mary Stevenson

Prayer for Light and Grace in the Choice of a State of Life

O my God,
you who are the God of wisdom and of counsel,
Who reads in my heart the sincere will
to please you alone, and to
govern myself with regard to my choice of
a state in life entirely in conformity
to your holy will, grant me, by the intercession
of the Most Blessed Virgin Mary, my mother,
and of my holy patrons, the grace to
know what state of life I ought to choose, and
when known to embrace it, so that in it I
may be able to pursue and increase your glory,
work out my salvation, and merit that
heavenly reward which you have promised
to those who do your will.   Amen.

Prayer to The Holy Spirit

HOLY Spirit, I want to do what is right.
                              – Help me.
Holy Spirit, I want to live like Jesus.   – Guide me.
Holy Spirit, I want to pray like Jesus. – Teach me.

Prayer for vocations to the Religious Life and Priesthood

O LORD Jesus Christ, who has said:
"The harvest indeed is great
but the labourers are few.
Pray therefore, to the Lord of the harvest
that he may send labourers into his harvest"
grant to members in our society the
gift of a vocation to the religious life
and priesthood. Grant them the grace
to accept your invitation and
the strength to fulfil their vocation that
they may do great things for God
and the salvation of the human family.

Reflection on Life

G OD has created me to do him
some definite service;
he has committed some work to me
which he has committed to no other.
I have my mission . . .
I am a link in a chain,
a bond of connection between persons.
He has not created me for naught.

Cardinal Newman

Thank You Lord

THAT I can see
   —so many are blind,
That I can hear
   —so many are deaf,
That I can walk
   —so many are disabled.
That I have food
   —so many are starving.
That I have shelter
   —so many are homeless.

For the touch of a friendly hand
   —so many are lonely.
For the cross you share with me
   and for all your blessings
      —so many deserve them better.
Help me always to be mindful.
                    Amen.

Prayer for Travellers

LOVING and merciful God,
When Abraham and Sarah left their own land,
you kept them safe.
You led the children of Israel on dry land,
parting the waters of the Red Sea.
You guided the Magi to your Son by a star.
Help us your children
that we may reach our destination in safety
and return home safe to our families and loved ones.
We ask this through Christ our Lord.

Iona Community Prayer

O God, for your love for us, warm and brooding,
 which has brought us to birth
and opened our eyes
to the wonder and beauty of creation.

WE GIVE YOU THANKS AND PRAISE

For your love for us, compassionate and patient,
which has carried us through our pain,
wept beside us in our sin,
and waited with us in our confusion.

WE GIVE YOU THANKS AND PRAISE

For your love for us, strong and challenging,
which has called us to risk for you,
asked for the best in us,
and shown us how to serve.

WE GIVE YOU THANKS AND PRAISE,
IN JESUS' NAME. AMEN

(Iona community, Scotland: adapted)

PRAYERS FOR FORGIVENESS

Our God is the God of compassion and mercy. The God who so loves us that he gave his only Son to die for our sins. The true prayer for forgiveness is born of the understanding of how much we owe to God's great mercy. Our Father is no angry God whom we must placate. He is, rather, an immense love to whom we must continually turn back from the self-centredness of our lives. To ask for forgiveness should mean that we are ready to allow God to create a new heart and a new spirit within us.

Act of Sorrow

O my God, I thank you for loving me.
I am sorry for all my sins,
for not loving others and not loving you.
Help me to live like Jesus and not sin again.
Amen.

PRAYERS TO OUR LADY

Some of the most ancient and beautiful christian prayers are addressed to the Mother of God. None, however, surpasses Mary's own great canticle—the Magnificat, (p. 14), which is the inspiration of many prayers to Our Lady. We give here a selection of the best known prayers to Mary including the latin version of the traditional antiphons to Our Lady.

Some of the prayers speak of Mary as Queen others as mother, and one addresses her as sister. This reminds us that Mary accompanies us on our journey through life. Pope Paul VI called Mary "our older sister in the faith".

Flos Carmeli
Carmelites' Prayer to Our Lady

F LOWER of Carmel,
    Tall vine, blossom laden,
Splendour of heaven,
Child-bearing, yet maiden,
None equals thee.

Mother so tender,
Who no man didst know,
On Carmel's children
Thy favour bestow.
Star of the Sea.

℣   Holy Mary, Mother of Christ, hear the cry of
your servants

℞   And bring down heavenly aid in answer to our
prayer.

Let us pray:

By a special privilege, Lord, you have adorned our
Order with the name of your Mother, the most
glorious Virgin Mary. Grant as we faithfully
remember this honour, that in these days we may
receive her protection and in the days to come we
may be brought to everlasting happiness. This we
ask of you who are living and reigning for ever.

Amen

Verses to Our Lady of Mount Carmel

℣ Blessed Virgin of Mount Carmel;
℟ Be our constant hope.

℣ Mary, perfect disciple of the Lord;
℟ Make us also faithful to him.

℣ Mary, Flower of Carmel;
℟ Fill us with your joy.

℣ Virgin Mary, Beauty of Carmel;
℟ Smile upon your family.

℣ Sweet Mother of Carmel;
℟ Accept me as your child.

℣ Mary, Mother beyond compare;
℟ Remember your children forever.

℣ Holy Virgin, Star of the Sea;
℟ Be our Beacon of Light.

℣ Protecting Veil;
℟ Shelter us in the mantle of your love.

℣ Mary, Conceived without sin;
℟ Pray for us who have recourse to you.

Let us pray:

O Father of all, look upon us as your children, and support us with your strength.
May we, who honour the memory of
Our Lady of Mount Carmel,
always rejoice in her unfailing protection.
Through Christ our Lord.   Amen.

Acclamations in honour of the Mother of Christ

1. Mary the Dawn, . . Christ the Perfect Day;
   Mary the Gate, . . Christ the Heavenly Way!

2. Mary the Root, . . Christ the Mystic Vine;
   Mary the Grape, . . Christ the Sacred Wine!

3. Mary the Stem, . . Christ the Rose, blood-red;
   Mary the Wheat, . . Christ the Living Bread!

4. Mary the Fount, . . Christ the Cleansing Flood;
   Mary the Cup, . . Christ the Saving Blood!

5. Mary the Temple, . . Christ the Temple's Lord;
   Mary the Shrine, . . Christ the God adored!

6. Mary the Beacon, . . Christ the haven's Rest;
   Mary the Mirror, . . Christ the Vision Blest!

7. Mary the Mother, . . Christ the Mother's Son;
   By all things bless'd while endless ages run!

Prayer for the Carmelite Family

TENDER hearted God,
   renew the gift of the Holy Spirit
   within the Carmelite Family
   as we seek to live following
   in the footsteps of Jesus Christ.
Teach us, like Mary, to contemplate your wisdom.
Fill us, like Elijah, with zeal for your glory.
Inspire us, like Simon Stock,
   to ponder your will in times of change.
Like Teresa, John, Thérèse and Titus,
   may we live always in your presence,
   and make us prophets of your Kingdom.
May our lives of prayer, community, and service
   be a sign to the world that God lives,
   in whose presence we stand.
This grace we ask in Jesus' name.
              Amen.

Prayer before an Icon of Our Lady of Mount Carmel

O God,
   you have given us Mary as our Mother
and, through the Order of Carmel,
we learn to call her sister.
May we imitate her goodness and faith,
and be ever joyful in the wonderful things
you have done for us.
May Mary watch over and protect us
on our pilgrim way to your holy mountain,
Christ the Lord.
We make our prayer through the same Christ,
Our Lord.   Amen.

Terenure College

THE angel of the Lord declared unto Mary:
and she conceived of the Holy Spirit.
Hail Mary . . .

Behold the handmaid of the Lord:
be it done to me according to your word.
Hail Mary . . .

And the Word was made flesh:
and dwelt among us.
Hail Mary . . .

℣ Pray for us, O holy mother of God.

℞ That we may be made worthy of the promises of Christ.

Let us pray:
Pour forth, we beseech you, O Lord, your grace into our hearts, that we to whom the incarnation of Christ, your Son, was made known by the message of an angel, may by his passion and cross be brought to the glory of his resurrection, through the same Christ our Lord.   Amen.

The Salve Regina

HAIL, Holy Queen, Mother of Mercy,
hail our life our sweetness and
our hope. To thee do we cry, poor
banished children of Eve:
to thee do we send up our sighs, mourning
and weeping in this vale of tears.
Turn then most gracious advocate,
thine eyes of mercy towards us;
and after this our exile,
show unto us the
blessed fruit of thy womb, Jesus.
O clement, O loving, O sweet Virgin Mary.

℣   Pray for us, O Holy Mother of God.

℟   That we may be made worthy of
the promises of Christ.

Let us pray:
Protect your servants, Lord, and keep us in peace.
As we trust in the intercession of the
Blessed Virgin Mary and all the saints,
keep us safe from every danger
and bring us to everlasting life
through Christ our Lord.   Amen.

Antiphon to Our Lady for Eastertime
(Regina Coeli)

O QUEEN of Heaven, rejoice;   Alleluia

For He Whom thou didst merit to bear;   Alleluia
Has risen, as he said: Alleluia
Pray for us to God;   Alleluia

℣   Rejoice and be glad, O Virgin Mary;
℞   For the Lord has risen indeed; Alleluia.

Let us pray,

O GOD, Who through the
      Resurrection of thy Son, Our Lord,
Jesus Christ,
was pleased to give joy to the world;
grant we beseech you, that through
His mother, the Virgin Mary, we may obtain
the joys of everlasting life.   Amen.

Memorare

REMEMBER, O most loving Virgin Mary,
that never was it known—
that anyone, who fled to your protection,
implored your help, or sought your intercession
        was left unaided.
Inspired with this confidence,
I fly unto you, O virgin of virgins my Mother,
To you do I come,
before you I stand, sinful and sorrowful.
O Mother of the Word Incarnate,
despise not my petitions, but in your clemency,
hear and answer me.   Amen.

St. Bernard (12th cent.)

Alma Redemptoris Mater

DEAR mother of our redeemer,
     ever-open gate of heaven,
star of the sea,
come to our help
as we fall and seek to rise again.
As all creation marvelled,
you gave birth to the Holy One
who created you.
Virgin maid and mother,
take to yourself the angel Gabriel's greeting
and have compassion on us sinners.

Ave, Regina coelorum

HAIL, Queen of heaven !
    Hail, Queen of angels !
Root of Jesse,
gate of heaven, hail !
From you light has risen on the world.
Rejoice, glorious virgin,
your beauty is unrivalled,
we greet your loveliness
and ask you to pray to Christ for us.

Dedication to Mary, our Mother

PRAY for us ever, Holy Mother of God,
   pray for us, whatever be our cross, as we pass
   along our way.
Pray for us, and we shall rise again,
   though we have fallen.

Pray for us when sorrow, anxiety or sickness comes
   upon us.
Pray for us when we are prostrate under the power
   of temptation.

Cardinal Newman

WHEN the storm of temptation arises
    When you are amidst the
reefs and shoals of tribulation
    Fix your gaze on the Star of the Sea.
        Call upon Mary.

Do the billows of anger; of avarice; lust
Batter against your soul—invoke Her name
In perils and sorrows and fears
    Fix your gaze on the Star of the Sea.
        Call upon Mary.

Under her protection, you shall know no fear—
Under her guidance, you shall not falter—
Under her patronage. you shall reach your goal.
    Fix your gaze on the Star of the Sea.
        Call upon Mary.

St. Bernard

Meditating day and night on the Law of the Lord and keeping vigil in prayer

Reflections on the Prayerful Reading of the Bible

A prayerful reading of the Bible within what is traditionally called *lectio divina* is an urgent task if we are to be faithful to what God asks of us today. It is something like curing the veins where the blood which keeps us alive has to flow. To this end we offer:

Ten words of advice about the mystical life which must guide our prayerful reading of the Bible; ie. the light which needs to be in our eyes when we do our *"lectio divina."*

Ten points of orientation (the least possible) for personal and daily reading of the Bible. Each person, will gradually develop his/her own way of communicating with the Word of God.

The Process of *"Lectio Divina"*
1. When you begin a *lectio divina* of the Bible you are not concerned with study; you are not going to read the Bible in order either to increase your knowledge or to prepare for some apostolate; you are not reading the Bible in order to have some extraordinary experience. You are going to read the Word of God in order to *listen* to what God has to say to you, to know His will

and thus "to live more deeply in allegiance to Jesus Christ" *(Carmelite Rule: Prologue)*. There must be poverty in you; you must also have the disposition which the old man Eli recommended to Samuel: "Speak, Lord, your servant is Listening" *(1Sam 3:10)*.

2. Listening to God does not depend on you or on the effort you make. It depends entirely on God, on his freely made decision to come into dialogue with you and to allow you to listen to his voice. Thus you need to *prepare yourself by asking him to send his Spirit,* since without the Spirit of God, it is impossible to discover the meaning of the Word which God has prepared for us today *(cf. Jn14:26; 16:13; Lk 11:13)*.

3. It is important to create *the right surroundings* which will facilitate recollection and an attentive listening to the Word of God. For this, you must build your cell within you and around you and you must stay in it *(Carmelite Rule: c VI)* all the time of your *lectio divina.* Putting one's body in the right position helps recollection in the mind.

4. When you open the Bible, you have to be conscious that you are opening a Book which is not yours. It belongs to *the community.* In your *lectio divina* you are setting foot in the great Tradition of the church which has come down through the centuries. Your prayerful reading is like the ship which carries down the winding river to the sea. The light shining from the sea has already enlightened the dark night of many generations.

In having your own experience of *lectio divina* you are not alone. You are united to brothers and sisters who before you succeeded in "meditating day and night upon the Law of the Lord and keeping vigil in prayer" *(Carmelite Rule: c VII)*.

5. An attentive and fruitful reading of the Bible involves three steps. It has to be marked, from beginning to end, by three attitudes:

First Step/Attitude — Reading: First of all, you have to ask, *"What does the text say as text?"* This requires that you *be silent*. Everything in you must be silent so that nothing stands in the way of your gleaning what the texts say to you *(Carmelite Rule: c XVI)* and so that you do not make the text say what you would like to hear.

Second Step/Attitude — Meditation: You must ask, *"What does the text say to me or to us?"* In this second step we enter into *dialogue* with the text so that its meaning comes across with freshness and penetrates the life of the Carmelite today. Like Mary you will ponder what you have heard and "meditate on the Law of the Lord?" *(VII)*. In this way "the Word of God, will dwell abundantly on your lips and in your heart" *(Carmelite Rule. c XIV)*.

Third Step/Attitude — Prayer: Furthermore you have to try to discover *"What does the text lead me to say to God?"* This is the moment of *prayer*, the moment of "keeping watch in prayer" *(Carmelite Rule c VII)*.

6. The result, the fourth step, the destination of *lectio divina*, is *contemplation*. Contemplation means having in one's eyes something of the "wisdom which leads to salvation" *(2Tm 3:15)*. We begin to see the world and life through the eyes of the poor, through the eyes of God. We assume our own poverty and eliminate from our way of thinking all that smacks of the powerful. We recognise all the many things which we thought were fidelity to God, to the Gospel, and to the Tradition of the Order; in reality they were nothing more than fidelity to ourselves and our own interests. We get a taste, even now, of the love of God which is above all things. We come to see that in our lives true love of God is revealed in love of our neighbour *(Carmelite Rule: c IX and XIV)*. It is like saying always, "let it be done to be according to your Word" *(LK 1:38)*. Thus "all you do will have the Lord's word for accompaniment" *(Carmelite Rule: c XIV)*.

7. So that your *lectio divina* does not end up being the conclusions of your own feelings, thoughts and caprices, but has the deepest roots, it is important to take account of *three demands:*

First Demand: *Check* the result of your reading *with the community* to which you belong *(Carmelite Rule: c XI)*, with the faith of the living Church. Otherwise it could happen that your effort might lead you nowhere *(cf. Gal 2:2)*.

Second Demand: Check what you read in the Bible *with what is going on in life around you*. It was in confronting its faith with the situation existing around them that the people of God created the traditions which up to today are visible in the Bible. The desire to embody the contemplative ideal of our Order within the reality of "minores" (the poor of each age) brought the first Carmelites to become mendicants. When the *lectio divina* does not reach its goal in our life, the reason is not always our failure to pray, our lack of attention to the faith of the church or our lack of serious study of the text. Oftentimes it is simply our failure to pay attention to the crude and naked reality which surrounds us. The early Christian writer, Cassian tells us that anyone who lives superficially, without seeking to go deeper, will not be able to reach the source where the Psalms were born.

Third Demand: *Check* the conclusions of your reading *with the results of biblical studies* which have shown the literal meaning of the words. *Lectio divina*, it has to be said, cannot remain chained to the letter. The Spirit's meaning has to be sought *(2Cor 3:6)*. However, any effort to identify the Spirit's meaning without basing it in the written word would be like trying to build a castle on sand (St. Augustine). That would be a way of falling into the trap of fundamentalism. In this day and age, when so many ideas are flying about, common sense is a most important quality. Common sense will be nourished by critical study of the written word. So that we will not go astray on this point, the Rule tells us to follow the example of the Apostle Paul *(Carmelite Rule: c XV)*.

8. The Apostle Paul gives various bits of advice on how to read the Bible. He himself was an excellent interpreter. Here are some of the norms and attitudes which he taught and followed:

When you set yourself to read the Bible:
(a) *Look upon yourself as the one to whom the word is addressed,* since everything was written for our instruction *(1Cor 10:11; Rom 15:4)*. The Bible is *our* book.

(b) *Keep faith in Jesus Christ in your eyes,* since it is only through faith in Jesus Christ that the veil is removed and the Scripture reveals its meaning and tells of that wisdom which leads to salvation *(2Cor 3:16; 2Tm 3:15; Rom 15:4)*.

(c) Remember how Paul spoke of *"Jesus Christ Crucified" (2Cor 2:2)*, a "stumbling block for some and foolishness for others". It was this Jesus who opened his eyes to see how, among the poor on the outskirts of Corinth, the foolishness and the stumbling block of the cross was confounding the wise, the strong and those who believed themselves to be something in this world *(1Cor 1:21-31)*.

(d) *Unite "I" and "we":* It is never a question of "I" alone or "we" alone. The Apostle also united the two. He received his mission from the community of Antioch and spoke from that background *(Acts 13:1-3)*.

(e) *Keep life's problems in mind:* All that is happening in the Carmelite Family, in the communities, in the church and among the people to which you belong and whom you serve. Paul began from what was going on in the communities which he founded *(1Cor 10:1-13).*

(9) When you read the Bible, be always aware that the text of the Bible is not only a fact. It is also a symbol *(Heb 11:19).* It is both a window through which you see what happened to others in the past and *a mirror in which you can see what is happening to you today (1Cor 10:6-10).* A prayerful reading is like a gentle flood which, little by little, waters the earth and makes it fruitful *(Is 55:10-11).* In beginning to dialogue with God in *lectio divina,* you grow like a tree planted near streams of water *(Ps 1:3).* You cannot see the growth but you can see its results in your encounter with yourself, with God and with others. The song says: "Like a flood that washes clean, like a fire that devours, so is your Word, leaving its mark upon me each time it passes."

(10) One final point to be born in mind: When you do a *lectio divina,* the principal object is not to interpret the Bible, nor to get to know its content, nor to increase your knowledge of the history of the People of God, nor to experience extraordinary things, but rather to *discover, with the help of the written Word, the living Word which God speaks to you today,* in your life, in our lives, in the life of the people, in the world in which we live *(Ps 97:5).* The purpose is to grow in faith, like

the prophet Elijah, and to experience more and more that "the Lord lives, and I stand in His presence" *(1Kg 17:1; 28:15).*

The Attitude of the Faithful Disciple

> "The Lord God has given me the tongue
> of those who are taught,
> that I may know how to sustain
> with a word the one that is weary."

> "Morning by morning, he wakens,
> he wakens my ear to hear
> as those who are taught."

1. Opening prayer, an invocation to the Holy Spirit.
2. Slow and attentive reading of the text.
3. A moment of interior silence, to recall what I have read.
4. Look at the meaning of each phrase.
5. Bring that word into the present, ponder it in relation to my life.
6. Broaden my vision by relating this text to other biblical texts.
7. Read the text again, prayerfully, giving a response to God.
8. Formulate my commitment in life.
9. Pray with a suitable psalm.
10. Choose a phrase which captures the meaning and memorise it.

"The Lord God has opened my ear,
and I was not rebellious,
I turned not backward.
I gave my back to the smiters,.....
For the Lord God helps me;
therefore I have set my face like a flint,
and I know that I shall not be
put to shame;
He who vindicates me is near".

(Is 50:4-8)

Carlos Mesters, O.Carm

Here are some suggested readings for Lectio Divina

Is 6: 1-9. I ... heard the voice of God saying: "Whom shall I send? ... And I said, "Here I am, send me."

Zep. 3: 14-20. Shout for joy ... exult with all your heart ... you have nothing more to fear ... he will renew you by his love.

Jer.1: 4-10. Before I formed you in the womb I knew you .. Do not be afraid ... Then they left everything and followed him.

Lk. 5: 1-11. ... Simon Peter fell at the knees of Jesus saying "Leave me Lord; I am a sinful man." But Jesus said, Do not be afraid ..." Then they left everything and followed him.

Lk. 8: 4-15. (Jesus) cried, "Anyone who has ears to hear should listen! ... people with a noble and generous heart who have heard the word and take it to themselves ... yield a harvest.

Jn. 1: 35-39. Jesus ... saw them following and said, "What do you want?" They answered "Where do you live?" He replied, "Come and see ..."

Rom. 12: 1-2. ... let the renewing of your minds transform you so that you may discern for yourselves what is the will of God ...

Jas. 5: 7-11. Now be patient ... do not lose heart, because our God's coming will be soon ... God is kind and compassionate.

1Thes. 5: 16-24. The one who called you is faithful.

C000180615

E
Country Churchyard
and other writings

THOMAS GRAY

A Phoenix Paperback
Poems, Letters and Essays by Thomas Gray first published by J.M. Dent in
1955
This edition first published in 1996 by Phoenix
a division of Orion Books Ltd
Orion House, 5 Upper St Martin's Lane, London WC2H 9EA

Copyright © Orion Books Ltd 1996

Cover illustration: 'The Magic Apple Tree' by Samuel Palmer, Fitzwilliam
Museum, University of Cambridge (Bridgeman Art Library, London)

All rights reserved. No part of this publication may be
reproduced, stored in a retrieval system, or transmitted,
in any form or by any means, electronic,
mechanical, photocopying, recording or otherwise,
without the prior permission of the copyright holder.

ISBN 1 85799 662 3

Typeset by Deltatype Ltd, Ellesmere Port, Cheshire
Printed in Great Britain by
Clays Ltd, St Ives plc.

Contents

Ode on a Distant
Prospect of Eton College

Ye distant spires, ye antique towers
   That crown the watery glade,
Where grateful Science still adores
   Her Henry's holy shade;
And ye, that from the stately brow
Of Windsor's heights th' expanse below
   Of grove, of lawn, of mead survey,
Whose turf, whose shade, whose flowers among
Wanders the hoary Thames along
   His silver-winding way:

Ah happy hills! ah pleasing shade!
   Ah fields beloved in vain!
Where once my careless childhood strayed,
   A stranger yet to pain!
I feel the gales that from ye blow
A momentary bliss bestow,
   As waving fresh their gladsome wing
My weary soul they seem to soothe,
And, redolent of joy and youth,
   To breathe a second spring.

Say, Father Thames, for thou hast seen
    Full many a sprightly race
Disporting on thy margent green
    The paths of pleasure trace;
Who foremost now delight to cleave
With pliant arm, thy glassy wave?
    The captive linnet which enthral?
What idle progeny succeed
To chase the rolling circle's speed
    Or urge the flying ball?

While some on earnest business bent
    Their murmuring labours ply
'Gainst graver hours, that bring constraint
    To sweeten liberty:
Some bold adventurers disdain
The limits of their little reign
    And unknown regions dare descry:
Still as they run they look behind,
They hear a voice in every wind,
    And snatch a fearful joy.

Gay hope is theirs by fancy fed,
    Less pleasing when possest;
The tear forgot as soon as shed,
    The sunshine of the breast:
Theirs buxom health, of rosy hue,
Wild wit, invention ever new,

And lively cheer, of vigour born;
The thoughtless day, the easy night,
The spirits pure, the slumbers light
   That fly th' approach of morn.

Alas! regardless of their doom
   The little victims play!
No sense have they of ills to come
   Nor care beyond to-day:
Yet see how all around them wait
The Ministers of human fate
   And black Misfortune's baleful train!
Ah show them where in ambush stand
To seize their prey, the murderous band!
   Ah, tell them they are men!

These shall the fury Passions tear,
   The vultures of the mind,
Disdainful Anger, pallid Fear,
   And Shame that skulks behind,
Or pining Love shall waste their youth;
Or Jealousy with rankling tooth
   That inly gnaws the secret heart,
And Envy wan, and faded Care,
Grim-visaged comfortless Despair,
   And Sorrow's piercing dart.

Ambition this shall tempt to rise,
    Then whirl the wretch from high,
To bitter Scorn a sacrifice
    And grinning Infamy.
The stings of Falsehood those shall try,
And hard Unkindness' altered eye,
    That mocks the tear it forced to flow;
And keen Remorse with blood defiled,
And moody Madness laughing wild
    Amid severest woe.

Lo, in the vale of years beneath
    A griesly troop are seen,
The painful family of Death,
    More hideous than their Queen:
This racks the joints, this fires the veins,
That every labouring sinew strains,
    Those in the deeper vitals rage:
Lo, Poverty, to fill the band,
That numbs the soul with icy hand,
    And slow-consuming Age.

To each his sufferings: all are men;
    Condemned alike to groan;
The tender for another's pain,
    Th' unfeeling for his own.
Yet, ah! why should they know their fate,

Since sorrow never comes too late,
  And happiness too swiftly flies?
Thought would destroy their paradise.
No more; – where ignorance is bliss,
  'Tis folly to be wise.

Elegy written in a Country Churchyard

The curfew tolls the knell of parting day,
  The lowing herd wind slowly o'er the lea,
The plowman homeward plods his weary way,
  And leaves the world to darkness and to me.

Now fades the glimmering landscape on the sight,
  And all the air a solemn stillness holds,
Save where the beetle wheels his droning flight,
  And drowsy tinklings lull the distant folds;

Save that from yonder ivy-mantled tower
  The moping owl does to the moon complain
Of such as, wand'ring near her secret bower,
  Molest her ancient solitary reign.

Beneath those rugged elms, that yew-tree's shade,
  Where heaves the turf in many a mould'ring heap,
Each in his narrow cell for ever laid,
  The rude forefathers of the hamlet sleep.

The breezy call of incense-breathing morn,
  The swallow twitt'ring from the straw-built shed,

The cock's shrill clarion, or the echoing horn,
  No more shall rouse them from their lowly bed.

For them no more the blazing hearth shall burn,
  Or busy housewife ply her evening care:
No children run to lisp their sire's return,
  Or climb his knees the envied kiss to share.

Oft did the harvest to their sickle yield,
  Their furrow oft the stubborn glebe has broke:
How jocund did they drive their team afield!
  How bowed the woods beneath their sturdy stroke!

Let not Ambition mock their useful toil,
  Their homely joys, and destiny obscure;
Nor Grandeur hear with a disdainful smile
  The short and simple annals of the poor.

The boast of heraldry, the pomp of power,
  And all that beauty, all that wealth e'er gave,
Awaits alike th' inevitable hour:
  The paths of glory lead but to the grave.

Nor you, ye proud, impute to These the fault,
  If Memory o'er their tomb no trophies raise,
Where through the long-drawn aisle and fretted vault
  The pealing anthem swells the note of praise.

Can storied urn or animated bust
    Back to its mansion call the fleeting breath?
Can Honour's voice provoke the silent dust,
    Or Flatt'ry soothe the dull cold ear of death?

Perhaps in this neglected spot is laid
    Some heart once pregnant with celestial fire;
Hands, that the rod of empire might have swayed,
    Or waked to ecstasy the living lyre.

But Knowledge to their eyes her ample page
    Rich with the spoils of time did ne'er unroll;
Chill Penury repressed their noble rage,
    And froze the genial current of the soul.

Full many a gem of purest ray serene
    The dark unfathomed caves of ocean bear;
Full many a flower is born to blush unseen,
    And waste its sweetness on the desert air.

Some village Hampden that with dauntless breast
    The little tyrant of his fields withstood,
Some mute inglorious Milton here may rest,
    Some Cromwell guiltless of his country's blood.

Th' applause of list'ning senates to command,
    The threats of pain and ruin to despise,
To scatter plenty o'er a smiling land,
    And read their history in a nation's eyes,

Their lot forbade: nor circumscribed alone
    Their growing virtues, but their crimes confined;
Forbade to wade through slaughter to a throne.
    And shut the gates of mercy on mankind,

The struggling pangs of conscious truth to hide,
    To quench the blushes of ingenuous shame,
Or heap the shrine of Luxury and Pride
    With incense kindled at the Muse's flame.

Far from the madding crowd's ignoble strife
    Their sober wishes never learned to stray;
Along the cool sequestered vale of life.
    They kept the noiseless tenor of their way.

Yet ev'n these bones from insult to protect
    Some frail memorial still erected nigh,
With uncouth rhymes and shapeless sculpture decked,
    Implores the passing tribute of a sigh.

Their name, their years, spelt by th' unlettered Muse,
    The place of fame and elegy supply:
And many a holy text around she strews,
    That teach the rustic moralist to die.

For who, to dumb Forgetfulness a prey,
    This pleasing anxious being e'er resigned,
Left the warm precincts of the cheerful day,
    Nor cast one longing ling'ring look behind?

On some fond breast the parting soul relies,
　　Some pious drops the closing eye requires;
E'en from the tomb the voice of Nature cries,
　　E'en in our Ashes live their wonted fires.

For thee, who, mindful of th' unhonoured dead,
　　Dost in these lines their artless tale relate;
If chance, by lonely contemplation led,
　　Some kindred spirit shall inquire thy fate,

Haply some hoary-headed Swain may say,
　　'Oft have we seen him at the peep of dawn
Brushing with hasty steps the dews away
　　To meet the sun upon the upland lawn.

'There at the foot of yonder nodding beech
　　That wreathes its old fantastic roots so high,
His listless length at noontide would he stretch,
　　And pore upon the brook that babbles by.

'Hard by yon wood, now smiling as in scorn,
　　Mutt'ring his wayward fancies he would rove,
Now drooping, woeful wan, like one forlorn,
　　Or crazed with care, or crossed in hopeless love.

'One morn I missed him on the customed hill,
　　Along the heath and near his fav'rite tree;
Another came; nor yet beside the rill,
　　Nor up the lawn, nor at the wood was he;

'The next with dirges due in sad array
    Slow through the church-way path we saw him borne.
Approach and read (for thou canst read) the lay
    Graved on the stone beneath yon aged thorn:'

The Epitaph

Here rests his head upon the lap of Earth
    A Youth to Fortune and to Fame unknown.
Fair Science frowned not on his humble birth,
    And Melancholy marked him for her own.

Large was his bounty, and his soul sincere,
    Heaven did a recompense as largely send:
He gave to Mis'ry all he had, a tear,
    He gained from Heaven ('twas all he wished) a friend.

No further seek his merits to disclose,
    Or draw his frailties from their dread abode,
(There they alike in trembling hope repose,)
The bosom, of his Father and his God.

The Bard

A Pindaric Ode

'Ruin seize thee, ruthless King!
   Confusion on thy banners wait!
Though fanned by Conquest's crimson wing
   They mock the air with idle state.
Helm, nor hauberk's twisted mail,
Nor e'en thy virtues, tyrant, shall avail
To save thy secret soul from nightly fears,
From Cambria's curse, from Cambria's tears!'
– Such were the sounds that o'er the crested pride
   Of the first Edward scattered wild dismay,
As down the steep of Snowdon's shaggy side
   He wound with toilsome march his long array: –
Stout Glo'ster stood aghast in speechless trance;
'To arms!' cried Mortimer, and crouched his quivering
     lance.

   On a rock, whose haughty brow
Frowns o'er old Conway's foaming flood,
   Robed in the sable garb of woe,
With haggard eyes the poet stood;
(Loose his beard and hoary hair

Streamed like a meteor to the troubled air;)
And with a master's hand and prophet's fire
Struck the deep sorrows of his lyre:
'Hark, how each giant oak and desert cave
    Sighs to the torrent's awful voice beneath!
O'er thee, O King! their hundred arms they wave
    Revenge on thee in hoarser murmurs breathe;
Vocal no more, since Cambria's fatal day,
To high-born Hoel's harp, or soft Llewellyn's lay.

'Cold is Cadwallo's tongue,
    That hushed the stormy main:
Brave Urien sleeps upon his craggy bed:
    Mountains, ye mourn in vain
    Modred, whose magic song
Made huge Plinlimmon bow his cloud-topt head.
    On dreary Arvon's shore they lie
Smeared with gore and ghastly pale:
Far, far aloof the affrighted ravens sail;
    The famished eagle screams, and passes by.
Dear lost companions of my tuneful art,
    Dear as the light that visits these sad eyes,
Dear as the ruddy drops that warm my heart,
    Ye died amidst your dying country's cries –
No more I weep. They do not sleep;
    On yonder cliffs, a griesly band,
I see them sit; they linger yet,
    Avengers of their native land:

With me in dreadful harmony they join;
And weave with bloody hands the tissue of thy line.

' "Weave the warp and weave the woof,
      The winding-sheet of Edward's race:
Give ample room and verge enough
      The characters of hell to trace.
Mark the year and mark the night
When Severn shall re-echo with affright
The shrieks of death through Berkley's roof that ring,
Shrieks of an agonizing king!
      She-wolf of France, with unrelenting fangs
That tear'st the bowels of thy mangled mate,
      From thee be born, who o'er thy country hangs
The scourge of heaven! What terrors round him wait!
Amazement in his van, with flight combined,
And sorrow's faded form, and solitude behind.

' "Mighty victor, mighty lord,
      Low on his funeral couch he lies!
No pitying heart, no eye, afford
      A tear to grace his obsequies.
Is the sable warrior fled?
Thy son is gone. He rests among the dead.
The swarm that in thy noon-tide beam were born?
– Gone to salute the rising morn.
Fair laughs the morn, and soft the zephyr blows,
      While proudly riding o'er the azure realm

In gallant trim the gilded vessel goes:
    Youth on the prow, and Pleasure at the helm:
Regardless of the sweeping whirlwind's sway,
That, hushed in grim repose, expects his evening prey.

' "Fill high the sparkling bowl,
The rich repast prepare;
    Reft of a crown, he yet may share the feast:
Close by the regal chair
    Fell Thirst and Famine scowl
    A baleful smile upon their baffled guest.
Heard ye the din of battle bray,
    Lance to lance, and horse to horse?
    Long years of havoc urge their destined course,
And through the kindred squadrons mow their way.
    Ye towers of Julius, London's lasting shame,
With many a foul and midnight murder fed,
    Revere his consort's faith, his father's fame,
And spare the meek usurper's holy head!
Above, below, the rose of snow,
    Twined with her blushing foe, we spread:
The bristled boar in infant-gore
    Wallows beneath the thorny shade.
Now, brothers, bending o'er the accursèd loom,
Stamp we our vengeance deep, and ratify his doom.

' "Edward, lo! to sudden fate
    (Weave we the woof; The thread is spun;)   15

Half of thy heart we consecrate.
    (The web is wove; The work is done.)"
Stay, O stay! nor thus forlorn
Leave me unblessed, unpitied, here to mourn:
In yon bright track that fires the western skies
They melt, they vanish from my eyes.
But O! what solemn scenes on Snowdon's height
    Descending slow their glittering skirts unroll?
Visions of glory, spare my aching sight,
    Ye unborn ages, crowd not on my soul!
No more our long-lost Arthur we bewail: –
All hail, ye genuine kings! Britannia's issue, hail!

    'Girt with many a baron bold
Sublime their starry fronts they rear;
    And gorgeous dames, and statesmen old
In bearded majesty, appear.
In the midst a form divine!
Her eye proclaims her of the Briton-line:
Her lion-port, her awe-commanding face
Attempered sweet to virgin-grace.
What strings symphonious tremble in the air,
    What strains of vocal transport round her play?
Hear from the grave, great Taliessin, hear;
    They breathe a soul to animate thy clay.
Bright Rapture calls, and soaring as she sings,
Waves in the eye of heaven her many-coloured wings.

'The verso adorn again
    Fierce war, and faithful love,
And Truth severe, by fairy Fiction drest.
    In buskined measures move
Pale grief, and pleasing pain,
With horror, tyrant of the throbbing breast.
A voice as of the cherub-choir
    Gales from blooming Eden bear,
    And distant warblings lessen on my ear,
That lost in long futurity expire.
Fond impious man, think'st thou yon sanguine cloud
    Raised by thy breath, has quenched the orb of day?
To-morrow he repairs the golden flood
    And warms the nations with redoubled ray.
Enough for me: with joy I see
    The different doom our fates assign:
Be thine despair and sceptred care;
    To triumph and to die are mine.'
– He spoke, and headlong from the mountain's height
Deep in the roaring tide he plunged to endless night.

The Progress of Poesy

A Pinaric Ode

Awake, Æolian, lyre, awake,
And give to rapture all thy trembling strings,
From Helicon's harmonious springs
  A thousand rills their mazy progress take:
The laughing flowers, that round them blow,
Drink life, and fragrance as they flow.
Now the rich stream of music winds along
Deep, majestic, smooth and strong,
Through verdant vales, and Ceres' golden reign:
Now rolling down the steep amain,
Headlong, impetuous, see it pour;
The rocks and nodding groves rebellow to the roar.

  O Sovereign of the willing soul,
Parent of sweet and solemn-breathing airs,
Enchanting shell! the sullen Cares
  And frantic Passions hear thy soft control.
On Thracia's hills the Lord of War
Has curbed the fury of his car,
And dropped his thirsty lance at thy command.
Perching on the sceptred hand

Of Jove, thy magic lulls the feathered king
With ruffled plumes and flagging wing:
Quenched in dark clouds of slumber lie
The terror of his beak, and lightnings of his eye.

Thee the voice, the dance, obey,
Tempered to thy warbled lay.
   O'er Idalia's velvet-green
   The rosy-crownèd Loves are seen
On Cytherea's day
   With antic Sports, and blue-eyed Pleasures,
   Frisking light in frolic measures;
Now pursuing, now retreating,
   Now in circling troops they meet:
To brisk notes in cadence beating,
   Glance their many-twinkling feet.
Slow melting strains their Queen's approach declare:
   Where'er she turns the Graces homage pay.
With arms sublime, that float upon the air,
   In gliding state she wins her easy way:
O'er her warm cheek and rising bosom move
The bloom of young Desire and purple light of Love.

   Man's feeble race what ills await,
Labour, and Penury, the racks of Pain,
   Disease, and Sorrow's weeping train,
   And Death, sad refuge from the storms of fate!
The fond complaint, my song, disprove,

And justify the laws of Jove.
Say, has he giv'n in vain the heav'nly Muse?
Night, and all her sickly dews,
Her spectres wan, and birds of boding cry,
He gives to range the dreary sky:
Till down the eastern cliffs afar
Hyperion's march they spy, and glitt'ring shafts of war.

    In climes beyond the solar road,
Where shaggy forms o'er ice-built mountains roam,
The Muse has broke the twilight gloom
    To cheer the shiv'ring native's dull abode.
And oft, beneath the odorous shade
Of Chili's boundless forests laid,
She deigns to hear the savage youth repeat
In loose numbers wildly sweet
Their feather-cinctured chiefs, and dusky loves.
Her track, where'er the Goddess roves,
Glory pursue and generous Shame,
Th' unconquerable Mind, and Freedom's holy flame.

Woods, that wave o'er Delphi's steep,
Isles, that crown th' Ægean deep,
    Fields, that cool Ilissus laves,
    Or where Maeander's amber waves
In lingering lab'rinths creep,
    How do your tuneful echoes languish,
    Mute, but to the voice of anguish?

Where each old poetic mountain
    Inspiration breathed around:
Every shade and hallowed fountain
    Murmured deep a solemn sound:
Till the Sad Nine, in Greece's evil hour,
    Left their Parnassus for the Latian plains.
Alike they scorn the pomp of tyrant Power,
    And coward Vice, that revels in her chains.
When Latium had her lofty spirit lost,
They sought, O Albion! next thy sea-encircled coast.

    Far from the sun and summer gale,
In thy green lap was Nature's darling laid,
What time, where lucid Avon strayed,
    To him the mighty mother did unveil
Her awful face: the dauntless child
Stretched forth his little arms, and smiled.
This pencil take (she said), whose colours clear
Richly paint the vernal year:
Thine too these golden keys, immortal boy!
This can unlock the gates of joy;
Of horror that, and thrilling fears,
Or ope the sacred source of sympathetic tears.

    Nor second he, that rode sublime
Upon the seraph-wings of Ecstasy,
The secrets of th' abyss to spy.
    He passed the flaming bounds of place and time:

The living throne, the sapphire-blaze,
Where angels tremble while they gaze,
He saw; but blasted with excess of light,
Closed his eyes in endless night.
Behold, where Dryden's less presumptuous car,
Wide o'er the fields of glory bear
Two coursers of ethereal race,
With necks in thunder clothed, and long-resounding pace.
Hark, his hands the lyre explore!
Bright-eyed Fancy hovering o'er
   Scatters from her pictured urn
   Thoughts that breathe, and words that burn.
But ah! 'tis heard no more –
   O lyre divine! what darling spirit
   Wakes thee now? Though he inherit
Nor the pride, nor ample pinion,
   That the Theban eagle bear
Sailing with supreme dominion
   Through the azure deep of air:
Yet oft before his infant eyes would run
   Such forms as glitter in the Muse's ray,
With orient hues, unborrowed of the sun:
   Yet shall he mount, and keep his distant way
Beyond the limits of a vulgar fate,
Beneath the Good how far – but far above the Great.

On a Favourite Cat, Drowned in a Tub of Gold Fishes

'Twas on a lofty vase's side,
Where China's gayest art had dyed
    The azure flowers that blow;
Demurest of the tabby kind,
The pensive Selima reclined,
    Gazed on the lake below.

Her conscious tail her joy declared;
The fair round face, the snowy beard,
    The velvet of her paws,
Her coat, that with the tortoise vies,
Her ears of jet, and emerald eyes,
    She saw; and purred applause.

Still had she gazed; but 'midst the tide
Two angel forms were seen to glide,
    The Genii of the stream:
Their scaly armour's Tyrian hue
Through richest purple to the view
    Betrayed a golden gleam.

The hapless Nymph with wonder saw:
A whisker first and then a claw,
    With many an ardent wish,
She stretched in vain to reach the prize.
What female heart can gold despise?
    What Cat's averse to fish?

Presumptuous Maid! with looks intent
Again she stretched, again she bent,
    Nor knew the gulf between.
(Malignant Fate sat by, and smiled.)
The slipp'ry verge her feet beguiled,
    She tumbled headlong in.

Eight times emerging from the flood
She mewed to every watery god,
    Some speedy aid to send.
No Dolphin came, no Nereid stirred:
Nor cruel *Tom*, nor *Susan* heard.
    A Fav'rite has no friend!

From hence, ye Beauties, undeceived,
Know, one false step is ne'er retrieved,
    And be with caution bold.
Not all that tempts your wand'ring eyes
And heedless hearts, is lawful prize;
    Nor all that glisters, gold.

The Triumphs of Owen

A Fragment

Owen's praise demands my song,
Owen swift, and Owen strong;
Fairest flower of Roderic's stem,
Gwyneth's shield, and Britain's gem
He nor heaps his brooded stores,
Nor on all profusely pours;
Lord of every regal art,
Liberal hand, and open heart.

Big with hosts of mighty name,
Squadrons three against him came;
This the force of Eirin hiding,
Side by side as proudly riding,
On her shadow long and gay
Lochlin plows the watery way;
There the Norman sails afar
Catch the winds, and join the war;
Black and huge along they sweep,
Burthens of the angry deep.

Dauntless on his native sands
The Dragon-Son of Mona stands;
In glitt'ring arms and glory dressed,
High he rears his ruby crest.
There the thund'ring strokes begin,
There the press, and there the din;
Talymaflra's rocky shore
Echoing to the battle's roar.
Where his glowing eye-balls turn,
Thousand banners round him burn.
Where he points his purple spear,
Hasty, hasty rout is there,
Marking with indignant eye
Fear to stop, and shame to fly
There confusion, terror's child,
Conflict fierce, and ruin wild,
Agony, that pants for breath,
Despair and honourable death.

Ode on the Pleasure Arising
from Vicissitude

Now the golden morn aloft
    Waves her dew-bespangled wing,
With vermeil cheek and whisper soft
    She woos the tardy spring:
Till April starts, and calls around
The sleeping fragrance from the ground;
And lightly o'er the living scene
Scatters his freshest, tenderest green.

New-born flocks in rustic dance
    Frisking ply their feeble feet.
Forgetful of their wintry trance
    The birds his presence greet.
But chief, the sky-lark warbles high
His trembling thrilling ecstasy
And, less'ning from the dazzled sight;
Melts into air and liquid light.

Yesterday the sullen year
    Saw the snowy whirlwind fly;
Mute was the music of the air,
    The herd stood drooping by:

Their raptures now that wildly flow,
No yesterday, nor morrow know;
'Tis man alone that joy descries
With forward and reverted eyes.

Smiles on past, Misfortune's brow
   Soft Reflection's hand can trace,
And o'er the cheek of Sorrow throw
   A melancholy grace;
While Hope prolongs our happier hour,
Or deepest shades, that dimly lour
And blacken round our weary way,
Gilds with a gleam of distant day.

Still, where rosy Pleasure leads,
   See a kindred grief pursue;
Behind the steps that Misery treads,
   Approaching Comfort view:
The hues of bliss more brightly glow,
Chastised by sabler tints of woe;
And blended form, with artful strife,
The strength and harmony of life.

See the wretch, that long has tossed
   On the thorny bed of pain,
At length repair his vigour lost,
   And breathe and walk again:
The meanest floweret of the vale,

The simplest note that swells the gale,
The common sun, the air, and skies,
To him are opening Paradise.

Stanzas to Mr Bentley

In silent gaze the tuneful choir among,
    Half pleased, half blushing, let the Muse admire,
While Bentley leads her sister-art along,
    And bids the pencil answer to the lyre.

See, in their course, each transitory thought
    Fixed by his touch a lasting essence take;
Each dream, in fancy's airy colouring wrought
    To local symmetry and life awake!

The tardy rhymes that used to linger on,
    To censure cold, and negligent of fame,
In swifter measures animated run,
    And catch a lustre from his genuine flame.

Ah! could they catch his strength, his easy grace,
    His quick creation, his unerring line;
The energy of Pope they might efface,
    And Dryden's harmony submit to mine.

But not to one in this benighted age
    Is that diviner inspiration given,
That burns in Shakespeare's or in Milton's page,
    The pomp and prodigality of heaven.

As, when conspiring in the diamond's blaze,
  The meaner gems, that singly charm the sight,
Together dart their intermingled rays,
  And dazzle with a luxury of light.

Enough for me, if to some feeling breast
  My lines a secret sympathy [impart;]
And as their pleasing influence [flows confest,]
  A sigh of soft reflection [heave the heart.]

Hymn of Adversity

Daughter of Jove, relentless power,
    Thou tamer of the human breast,
Whose iron scourge and torturing hour
    The bad affright, afflict the best!
Bound in thy adamantine chain
The proud are taught to taste of pain,
And purple tyrants vainly groan
With pangs unfelt before, unpitied and alone.

When first thy Sire to send on earth
    Virtue, his darling child, designed,
To thee he gave the heavenly birth
    And bade to form her infant mind.
Stern, rugged Nurse! thy rigid lore
With patience many a year she bore:
What sorrow was, thou bad'st her know,
And from her own she learned to melt at others' woe.

Scared at thy frown terrific, fly
    Self-pleasing Folly's idle brood,
Wild Laughter, Noise, and thoughtless Joy,
    And leave us leisure to be good.
Light they disperse, and with them go
The summer Friend, the flattering Foe;

By vain Prosperity received,
To her they vow their truth, and are again believed.

Wisdom in sable garb arrayed
    Immersed in rapturous thought profound,
And Melancholy, silent maid,
    With leaden eye, that loves the ground,
Still on thy solemn steps attend;
Warm Charity, the general friend,
With Justice, to herself severe,
And Pity dropping soft the sadly-pleasing tear.

O, gently on thy suppliant's head,
    Dread Goddess, lay thy chastening hand!
Not in thy Gorgon terrors clad,
    Nor circled with the vengeful band
(As by the impious thou art seen)
With thundering voice, and threatening mien,
With screaming Horror's funeral cry,
Despair, and fell Disease, and ghastly Poverty;

Thy form benign, O Goddess, wear,
    Thy milder influence impart,
Thy philosophic train be there
    To soften, not to wound my heart.
The generous spark extinct revive,
Teach me to love and to forgive,
Teach my own defects to scan,
What others are to feel, and know myself a Man.

Ode on the Spring

Lo! where the rosy-bosomed Hours,
   Fair Venus' train, appear,
Disclose the long-expecting flowers
   And wake the purple year!
The Attic warbler pours her throat
Responsive to the cuckoo's note,
The untaught harmony of Spring:
   While, whispering pleasure as they fly,
   Cool Zephyrs through the clear blue sky
Their gathered fragrance fling.

Where'er the oak's thick branches stretch
   A broader, browner shade,
Where'er the rude and moss-grown beech
   O'er-canopies the glade,
Beside some water's rushy brink
With me the Muse shall sit, and think
(At ease reclined in rustic state)
   How vain the ardour of the Crowd;
   How low, how little are the Proud,
How indigent the Great!

Still is the toiling hand of Care;
    The panting herds repose:
Yet hark, how through the peopled air
    The busy murmur glows!
The insect youth are on the wing,
Eager to taste the honied spring
And float amid the liquid noon:
    Some lightly o'er the current skim,
    Some show their gaily-gilded trim
Quick-glancing to the sun.

To Contemplation's sober eye
    Such is the race of Man:
And they that creep, and they that fly,
    Shall end where they began.
Alike the busy and the gay
But flutter through life's little day,
In Fortune's varying colours dressed:
    Brushed by the hand of rough Mischance,
    Or chilled by Age, their airy dance
They leave, in dust to rest.

Methinks I hear in accents low
    The sportive kind reply:
Poor moralist! and what art thou?
    A solitary fly!
Thy joys no glittering female meets,
No hive hast thou of hoarded sweets,

No painted plumage to display:
　　On hasty wings thy youth is flown;
　　Thy sun is set, thy spring is gone –
We frolic while 'tis May.

Sketch of His Own Character

Written in 1761,
and Found in One of His Pocket-Books.

Too poor for a bribe, and too proud to importune;
He had not the method of making a fortune:
Could love, and could hate, so was thought somewhat odd;
No very great wit, he believ'd in a God:
A post or a pension he did not desire,
But left church and state to Charles Townshend and Squire.

Amatory Lines

With beauty, with pleasure surrounded, to languish –
To weep without knowing the cause of my anguish:
To start from short slumbers, and wish for the morning –
To close my dull eyes when I see it returning;
Sighs sudden and frequent, looks dejected –
Words that steal from my tongue, by no meaning
    connected!
Ah, say, fellow-swains, how these symptoms befell me?
They smile, but reply not – Sure Delia will tell me!

Song

Thyrsis, when we parted, swore
   Ere the spring he would return –
Ah! what means yon violet flower!
   And the bud that decks the thorn!
'Twas the lark that upward sprung!
'Twas the nightingale that sung!

Idle notes! untimely green!
   Why this unavailing haste?
Western gales and skies serene
   Speak not always winter past.
Cease, my doubts, my fears to move,
Spare the honour of my love.

The Descent of Odin

From the Norse Tongue

Up rose the King of men with speed,
And saddled straight his coal-black steed;
Down the yawning steep he rode,
That leads to Hela's drear adobe.
Him the Dog of Darkness spied,
His shaggy throat he open'd wide,
While from his jaws, with carnage fill'd,
Foam and human gore distill'd:
Hoarse he bays with hideous din,
Eyes that glow, and fangs that grin;
And long pursues, with fruitless yell,
The father of the powerful spell.
Onward still his way he takes,
(The groaning earth beneath him shakes,)
Till full before his fearless eyes
The portals nine of hell arise.

　　Right against the eastern gate,
By the moss-grown pile he sate;
Where long of yore to sleep was laid
The dust of the prophetic maid.

Facing to the northern clime,
Thrice he trac'd the Runic rhyme;
Thrice pronounc'd in accents dread
The thrilling verse that wakes the dead;
Till from out the hollow ground
Slowly breath'd a sullen sound.

PR.   What call unknown, what charms presume
To break the quiet of the tomb?
Who thus afflicts my troubled sprite,
And drags me from the realms of night?
Long on these mould'ring bones have beat
The winter's snow, the summer's heat,
The drenching dews, and driving rain!
Let me, let me sleep again.
Who is he, with voice unblest,
That calls me from the bed of rest?

O.   A traveller, to thee unknown,
Is he that calls, a warrior's son.
Thou the deeds of light shalt know;
Tell me what is done below,
For whom yon glitt'ring board is spread,
Drest for whom yon golden bed.

PR.   Mantling in the goblet see
The pure bev'rage of the bee;
O'er it hangs the shield of gold;

'Tis the drink of Balder bold:
Balder's head to death is giv'n.
Pain can reach the sons of heav'n!
Unwilling I my lips unclose:
Leave me, leave me to repose.

   O.   Once again my call obey.
Prophetess, arise, and say,
What dangers Odin's child await,
Who the author of his fate.

   Pr.   In Hoder's hand the hero's doom:
His brother sends him to the tomb.
Now my weary lips I close:
Leave me, leave me to repose.

   O.   Prophetess, my spell obey,
Once again arise, and say,
Who th' avenger of his guilt,
By whom shall Hoder's blood be spilt.

   Pr.   In the caverns of the west,
By Odin's fierce embrace comprest,
A wondrous boy shall Rinda bear,
Who ne'er shall comb his raven-hair,
Nor wash his visage in the stream,
Nor see the sun's departing beam;
Till he on Hoder's corse shall smile

Flaming on the fun'ral pile.
Now my weary lips I close:
Leave me, leave me to repose.

    O. Yet awhile my call obey.
Prophetess, awake, and say,
What virgins these, in speechless woe,
That bend to earth their solemn brow,
That their flaxen tresses tear,
And snowy veils, that float in air.
Tell me whence their sorrows rose:
Then I leave thee to repose.

    PR.   Ha! no traveller art thou,
King of men, I know thee now,
Mightiest of a mighty line –

    O.   No boding maid of skill divine
Art thou, nor prophetess of good;
But mother of the giant-brood!

PR.   Hie thee hence, and boast at home,
That never shall inquirer come
To break my iron-sleep again;
Till Lok has burst his tenfold chain.
Never, till substantial Night
Has reassum'd her ancient right;
Till wrapp'd in flames, in ruin hurl'd,
Sinks the fabric of the world.

Mr Gray to Mr Walpole

Compliment of condolence on the death of his favourite cat, enclosing his Ode upon that subject.

Cambridge, 1 March, 1747

As one ought to be particularly careful to avoid blunders in a compliment of condolence, it would be a sensible satisfaction to me (before I testify my sorrow, and the sincere part I take in your misfortune) to know for certain, who it is I lament. I knew Zara and Selima, (Selima, was it? or Fatima) or rather I knew them both together; for I cannot justly say which was which. Then as to your handsome cat, the name you distinguish her by, I am no less at a loss, as well knowing one's handsome cat is always the cat one likes best; or, if one be alive and the other dead, it is usually the latter that is the handsomest. Besides, if the point were never so clear, I hope you do not think me so ill-bred or so imprudent as to forfeit all my interest in the survivor: Oh no! I would rather seem to mistake, and imagine to be sure it must be the tabby one that had met with this sad accident. Till this affair is a little better determined, you will excuse me if I do not begin to cry:

44

'Tempus inane peto, requiem, spatiumque doloris.'

Which interval is the more convenient, as it gives time to rejoice with you on your new honours. This is only a beginning; I reckon next week we shall hear you are a Freemason, or a Gormogon at least – Heigh ho! I feel, (as you to be sure have done long since) that I have very little to say, at least in prose. Somebody will be the better for it; I do not mean you, but your cat, *feuë Mademoiselle Selime*, whom I am about to immortalize for one week or fortnight, as follows [. . .]

There's a poem for you, it is rather too long for an epitaph.

Mr Gray to Dr Wharton

*On the ill reception which Gray's poem 'Long Story' met
with in town when handed about in manuscript, and how
much his Elegy in a Country Churchyard was applauded.*

17 December, 1750

Of my house I cannot say much, I wish I could; but for my
heart it is no less yours than it has long been; and the last
thing in the world that will throw it into tumults is a fine
lady. The verses, you so kindly try to keep in countenance,
were written merely to divert Lady Cobham and her family,
and succeeded accordingly; but being shewed about in
town are not liked there at all. Mrs—, a very fashionable
personage, told Mr Walpole that she had seen a thing by a
friend of his which she did not know what to make of, for it
aimed at every thing, and meant nothing; to which he
replied, that he had always taken her for a woman of sense,
and was very sorry to be undeceived. On the other hand, the
stanzas which I now inclose to you have had the misfortune,
by Mr Walpole's fault, to be made still more public, for
which they certainly were never meant; but it is too late to
complain. They have been so applauded, it is quite a shame
to repeat it: I mean not to be modest; but it is a shame for

46

those who have said such superlative things about them, that I cannot repeat them. I should have been glad that you and two or three more people had liked them, which would have satisfied my ambition on this head amply. I have been this month in town, not at Newcastle-house; but diverting myself among my gay acquaintance, and return to my cell with so much the more pleasure. I dare not speak of my future excursion to Durham for fear of a disappointment, but at present it is my full intention.

Mr Gray to Mr Walpole

Desires Mr Walpole to give his Elegy to Mr Dodsley to be printed immediately, in order to prevent its publication in a magazine.

Cambridge, 11 February, 1751

As you have brought me into a little sort of distress, you must assist me, I believe, to get out of it as well as I can. Yesterday I had the misfortune of receiving a letter from certain gentlemen (as their bookseller expresses it,) who have taken the Magazine of Magazines into their hands: they tell me that an *ingenious* Poem, called Reflections in a Country Churchyard, has been communicated to them, which they are printing forthwith; that they are informed that the *excellent* author of it is I by name, and that they beg not only his *indulgence*, but the *honour* of his correspondence, &c. As I am not at all disposed to be either so indulgent, or so correspondent, as they desire, I have but one bad way left to escape the honour they would inflict upon me; and therefore am obliged to desire you would make Dodsley print it immediately (which may be done in less than a week's time) from your copy, but without my name, in what form is most convenient for him, but on his

48

best paper and character; he must correct the press himself, and print it without any interval between the stanzas, because the sense is in some places continued beyond them; and the title must be – 'Elegy, written in a Country Churchyard'. If he would add a line or two to say it came into his hands by accident, I should like it better. If you behold the Magazine of Magazines in the light that I do, you will not refuse to give yourself this trouble on my account, which you have taken of your own accord before now. If Dodsley do not do this immediately, he may as well let it alone.

Mr Gray to Dr Wharton

Objection to publishing his Ode on the Progress of Poetry singly. Hint of his having other unfinished lyrical ideas.

Cambridge, 9 March, 1755

I do not pretend to humble any one's pride; I love my own too well to attempt it. As to mortifying their vanity, it is too easy and too mean a task for me to delight in. You are very good in shewing so much sensibility on my account: but be assured my taste for praise is not like that of children for fruit; if there were nothing but medlars and black-berries in the world, I could be very well content to go without any at all. I dare say that Mason, though some years younger than I, was as little elevated with the approbation of Lord—and Lord—, as I am mortified by their silence.

With regard to publishing, I am not so much against the thing itself, as of publishing this Ode alone. I have two or three ideas more in my head; what is to come of them? must they too come out in the shape of little sixpenny flams, dropping one after another till Mr Dodsley thinks fit to collect them with Mr This's Song, and Mr Tother's Epigram, into a pretty volume? I am sure Mason must be sensible of this, and therefore cannot mean what he says;

50

neither am I quite of your opinion with regard to strophe and antistrophe; setting aside the difficulty of execution methinks it has little or no effect on the ear, which scarce perceives the regular return of metres at so great a distance from one another: to make it succeed, I am persuaded the stanzas must not consist of above nine lines each at the most. Pindar has several such odes.

Mr Gray to Mr Hurd

On the ill reception his two Pindaric Odes met with on their publication.

Stoke, 25 August, 1757

I do not know why you should thank me for what you had a right and title to; but attribute it to the excess of your politeness; and the more so, because almost no one else has made me the same compliment. As your acquaintance in the University (you say) do me the honour to *admire*, it would be ungenerous in me not to give them notice, that they are doing a very unfashionable thing; for all people of condition are agreed not to admire, nor even to understand. One very great man, writing to an acquaintance of his and mine, says that he had read them seven or eight times; and that now, when he next sees him, he shall not have above *thirty questions* to ask. Another (a peer) believes that the last stanza of the second ode relates to King Charles the First and Oliver Cromwell. Even my friends tell me they do not *succeed*, and write me moving topics of consolation on that head. In short, I have heard of nobody but an actor and a doctor of divinity that profess their esteem for them. Oh yes, a lady of quality, (a friend of Mason's) who is a great reader. She knew there was a compliment to Dryden, but never suspected there was any thing said about Shakespeare or Milton, till it was explained to her; and wishes that there had been titles prefixed to tell what they were about.

From this mention of Mason's name you may think, perhaps, we are great correspondents. No such thing; I have not heard from him these two months. I will be sure to scold in my own name, as well as in yours. I rejoice to hear you are so ripe for the press, and so voluminous; not for my own sake only, whom you flatter with the hopes of seeing your labours, both public and private, but for yours too; for to be employed is to be happy. This principle of mine (and I am convinced of its truth) has, as usual, no influence on my practice. I am alone, and *ennuyé* to the last degree, yet do nothing. Indeed I have one excuse; my health (which you have so kindly inquired after) is not extraordinary, ever since I came hither. It is no great malady, but several little ones, that seem brewing no good to me. It will be a particular pleasure to me to hear whether Content dwells in Leicestershire, and how she entertains herself there. Only do not be too happy, nor forget entirely the quiet ugliness of Cambridge.

Mr Gray to Dr Wharton

From a journal of his tour through Westmoreland, Cumberland, and a part of Yorkshire.

1 October

A grey autumnal day, the air perfectly calm and mild, went to see Ulswater, five miles distant; soon left the Keswick road, and turned to the left through shady lanes along the vale of Eeman, which runs rapidly on near the way, ripling over the stones; to the right is Delmaine, a large fabrick of pale red stone, with nine windows in front and seven on the side, built by Mr Hassle, behind it a fine lawn surrounded by woods, and a long rocky eminence rising over them: a clear and brisk rivulet runs by the house to join the Eeman, whose course is in sight and at a small distance. Farther on appears Hatton St John, a castle-like old mansion of Mr Huddleston. Approached Dunmallert, a fine-pointed hill covered with wood, planted by old Mr Hassle before-mentioned, who lives always at home and delights in planting. Walked over a spungy meadow or two, and began to mount the hill through a broad straight green alley among the trees, and with some toil gained the summit. From hence saw the lake opening directly at my feet, majestic in its calmness, clear and smooth as a blue mirror, with winding shores and low points of land covered with green inclosures, white farm-houses looking out among the trees, and cattle feeding. The water is almost every where bordered with cultivated lands, gently sloping upwards from a mile to a quarter of a mile in breadth, till they reach the feet of the mountains, which rise very rude and awful with their broken tops on either hand. Directly in front, at better than three miles distance, Place Fell, one of the bravest among them, pushes its bold broad breast into the midst of the lake, and forces it to alter its course, forming first a large bay to the left, and then bending to the right. I descended Dunmallert again by a side avenue that was only not perpendicular; and came to Barton-bridge over the Eeman; then walking through a path in the wood round the bottom of the hill, came forth where the Eeman issues out of the lake, and continued my way along its western shore close to the water, and generally on a level with it. Saw a cormorant flying over it and fishing. The figure of the lake nothing resembles that laid down in our maps; it is nine miles long; and at widest under a mile in breadth. After extending itself three miles and a half in a line to south-west, it turns at the foot of Place Fell almost due west, and is here not twice the breadth of the Thames at London. It is soon again interrupted by the root of Helvellyn, a lofty and very rugged mountain, and spreading again turns off to south-east, and is lost among the deep recesses of the hills.

3 October.   A heavenly day; the grass was covered with

a hoarfrost, which soon melted and exhaled in a thin bluish smoke; crossed the meadows, obliquely catching a diversity of views among the hills over the lake and islands, and changing prospect at every ten paces . . .

This scene continues to Barrowgate; and a little farther, passing a brook called Barrow-beck, we entered Borrow-dale: the crags named Lawdoor-banks begin now to impend terribly over your way, and more terribly when you hear that three years since an immense mass of rock tumbled at once from the brow and barred all access to the dale (for this is the only road) till they could work their way through it. Luckily no one was passing at the time of this fall; but down the side of the mountain, and far into the lake, lie dispersed the huge fragments of this ruin in all shapes and in all directions: something farther we turned aside into a coppice, ascending a little in front of Lawdoor water-fall; the height appeared to be about two hundred feet, the quantity of water not great, though (these three days excepted) it had rained daily in the hills for near two months before; but then the stream was nobly broken, leaping from rock to rock, and foaming with fury. On one side a towering crag that spired up to equal, if not overtop the neighbouring cliffs (this lay all in shade and darkness): on the other hand a rounder broader projecting hill shagged with wood, and illuminated by the sun, which glanced sideways on the upper part of the cataract. The force of the water wearing a deep channel in the ground, hurries away to join the lake. We descended again and passed the stream over a rude bridge. Soon after we came under Gowdar-crag, a hill more formidable to the eye, and to the apprehension, than that of Lawdoor; the rocks at top deep-cloven perpendicularly, by the rains, hanging loose and nodding forwards, seem just starting from their base in shivers. The whole way down and the road on both sides is strewed with piles of the fragments strangely thrown across each other, and of a dreadful bulk: the place reminds me of those passes in the Alps, where the guides tell you to move on with speed, and say nothing, least the agitation of air should loosen the snows above, and bring down a mass that would overwhelm a caravan. I took their counsel here and hastened on in silence.

Non ragioniam di lor, ma guarda, e passa!

A Note on Thomas Gray

Thomas Gray (1716–71), the English poet, was born in London, the son of a scrivener whose cruelty and violence forced his wife to separate from him. Gray's mother and sister ran a millinery business which enabled him to be sent to Eton (where he became a friend of Horace Walpole) and Peterhouse, Cambridge. A studious and reserved man, the story of his life is simple and colourless, its outstanding event being his tour on the Continent with Horace Walpole, 1739–41. Their unfortunate quarrel, late in this tour, which was not healed for three years, was the only break in a lifelong friendship.

Returning to England, Gray found his father dying and his mother only moderately provided for. After living with her for a while at Stoke Poges he went back to Cambridge where, except for brief intervals, he spent the rest of his life. There he settled in Peterhouse, later transferring himself to Pembroke College. Gray always had a tendency towards melancholy yet he was mostly very humorous, and his letters, charming in their mixture of fun, sincere friendliness, and perceptive criticism of men and books, rank with those of Charles Lamb. His learning was immense, not only in the classics (his early verse was written in Latin) but also in Celtic and Old Norse, art, and natural sciences. Among his best poems are 'Ode on the Spring'; 'Hymn to Adversity'; 'Ode on a Distant Prospect of Eton College'; 'Sonnet on the Death of Mr Richard West', commemorating the death of his close friend; and the famous 'Elegy written in a Country Churchyard', 1751. The 'Elegy', begun ten years earlier, was instantly acclaimed and the work, with its dignified contemplation of death, expressed in disciplined language, is one of the most familiar of English poems.

Gray's works are few in number and in quality fail to reach the highest rank, even the immortal 'Elegy' owing its fame to exquisite expression and natural pathos rather than to great or original thought. Nor were all his poems admired by his contemporaries; the Odes, 'The Progress of Poesy', and 'The Bard' were criticised by Samuel Johnson, among others, as obscure. However, if the 'Elegy', the Odes, and the translations from the Norse are compared with anything written by his immediate predecessors (except Thomson), it will be seen that Gray was a pioneer, a key figure in a transitional period, and the forerunner of Goldsmith and Cowper in developing a style markedly different from that of the poetically dominant Alexander Pope.

Gray was one of the first to celebrate the glories of mountain scenery. While other writers were still shuddering at 'horrid precipices' and 'frightful solitudes' he was enthusiastic in his admiration of the Alps, and later of the Grampian and Cumbrian peaks. In this he was a precursor of the Romantics.